WORD BATH

WORD BATH

Kassie Duke

ISBN (print): 978-0-578-34745-5
ISBN (eBook): 978-0-578-34746-2

Cover art by Kayla Allen
Typesetting by C'est Beau Designs

CONTENTS

"Life is titleless," she thought, lying under the oak.
"Yes, that's the sort of ~deep~ thing they mean."
A bird bustled above.
"This is going to take all of my energy, isn't it?"
She was speaking only to the air.
"I want to bathe in all of this... but how?
And why would anyone listen?"

Her soles grew warm in the sun.

i.

NOT ABOUT LOVE

She said to herself,
"I think I'll sit here awhile...
and think about something else."
And the wind whispered back, "What an idea."

In a while, I won't be ice anymore;

able to melt with the murmur of a warm breath.

I'll be a river running, moving with the might of the wind.

The spring of my soul will wash away the flows floating down

  stream

and I will dream— not of the time I spent in winter—

but of the sun coming up with the steam.

I stirred a spot of sunshine into my tea.

It fell from above on an otherwise rainy day

and tempered the tempest as it steeped deeply.

I sipped and savored the sweetness

cut with clouds of milk.

I wished I could capture the sunlight

and swirl it in my mouth

until the beams shot out of my eyes

and hugged my hips so tightly,

I knew it would never leave.

But rays weren't meant to stay

kept in a porcelain cup,

but savored in a silent space so

the sensation shoots through you

and out just as quickly as it came;

to thrill the rest of the world with

its brightness.

The scratches on the wall are slowly fading

marks made to move memories to tears;

drying into salt on puffs of skin. Cracked riverbeds.

Dents left on an arm held for a long length of time: Gone.

Beyond the bed where half-love had lain, scent dissipates...

and eyes wake at all hours and when weeks have been made

  into months

breath becomes easy again. Fresh air fills the lungs—

sunlight spills into strands of hair

and the chest cavity feels the gravity of then, and the newness

  of now,

and the wonder of what may.

Not About Love

Rain drops fell and woke me while I slept.

I dreamt it was then and then another time.

And when I went to sleep again the droplets

came again to wake me... pitter-patter, pit-pat.

I asked the mountain how much farther I should go
and it said, "Still higher."

 Not About Love

When I woke on the last day of my life
I told my children: Lay me in a mountain.
Tell the great, Dark King to ring the bells
and mourn my loss in a cavern deep.
Write ballads of my bravery, emblazon
them on the rooftops until they're faded and gone
and all that's left are songs; sweet singing
lullabies of old days on the day that I died.

I carved this one out from the bottom of my brain

where the stew sits brewing in a hot pool of steam

and thick, molten liquid; churning ash falling from above.

Where I steep my feet to think and swirl the water

around my ankles to create different designs

and try to see something in them.

Maybe my future, maybe my past,

and maybe something that will last.

But I go back here, in the middle of my day,

when I can't think of anything to say to smiling faces.

I sit and watch my ankles turn red, burn to bone.

And regrow the skin the next day.

I wonder what the end of the earth looks like

Is it a small shelter on the edge of a ruin

a snow-capped cliff jutting straight into the sky

or a silent cemetery where ancestors lie

Is there love at the end of it all

cupped in a child's hands and warmed

with the breath of my sigh

Is there ecstasy-high and low light of nights

the ones where we create life

and do we dance with our arms around each other

long into the after of life in the ethereal

Do we carry on conversations or are we done

Is there only staring into space caught in our eyes

What wonder it must be to see wrapped in crystal glass

all the what-ifs in the ends of the earth

trapped in the ceilings of skies

I swore the sound of crashing waves awoke me

but it wasn't

silly me

just the bang of a book as it fell from my bed to the floor

a paperback pressed in my hands while I nodded off

I turned and prayed that when I closed my eyes again

I'd feel the tide rising

lapping at my feet

salty seas shoring while I sleep

for I am so far from the ocean

I only see it in my dreams

These white, wispy flecks in the air;

thoughts falling in piles on

these streets I perceive.

Here is that scene

tipped with pricks of pristine

gleaming, glowing, bright

shards of light;

bouncing from the banks

and reflecting into the

eyes of passersby.

Strangers to the cold,

walking with wishes

held beneath layers of wool.

I heard shouting from the inside of a locked door

interspersed with bursts of painful screams

I wasn't the keeper of the keys

and so I stood pacing outside

wondering what was happening behind

I begged to be let in

my worries far out-reaching the reality when

it opened and I saw someone

sitting and smiling

as if nothing had happened

and I don't think she saw it

the shadow on the ceiling

lurking over her

a finger to its lips

The rain wept in sheets;

a low lament bellowing

the groan of a gong.

Many are the months of rain.

Green is the grass, slow growing.

my hand caught the wind

and I tamed it to a breeze

mellowed by my palm

Not About Love

A salty old sailor— with the wealth of the world in his eyes.

Made hard by the waves washing over the decks of

warped wood, packed tight with tar in the crevices;

dry and cracked from the sunlight of the sea.

Only sails for shelter on that everlasting glass surface.

Sand is the skin on his hands, tides the torrent of his heart.

Long were his days bathed in cold air.

Softly, still, falls his step on the shore.

Did the sand drip out,

and is the hour now late;

too empty to tell the time?

                    Not About Love

I undressed

my expectations

and saw

a small,

simple heart

still beating.

"I always

thought

it would be

more— red."

I said.

"Fire and

fierceness.

Never a

shade so

pink.

Plain,

but lovely,

I think."

maybe now is when we'll see

the driest flowers smell as sweet

these old October growths

Not About Love

ii.

NOT ABOUT LOSS

∞

"I can only sit here for so long," she said.

"Before I start to feel it in my back."

"Then," said the sparrow. "You should run around a bit."

The fire burns hot at the hearth inside

and the wind blows swiftly through dead leaves.

The oak bed posts lean and creak.

Still, the wind rattles the shutters,

but nothing can be seen.

Cold glass, warmed with steam.

ROMANTICIZE.

Love me like the one in an old, western film;

Walk with a stride I can measure in breaths,

slow and straight and tall and bold in your broad

gait. Go down to the edge of town to set right

a wrong wrought from a twisted, lawless brawl.

Be a harbinger of justice while I watch you from

the window of a saloon and you steal the town

with your stoicism, inciting whispers of mystery.

Let me wonder at what brought you to my

stoop to stay when you wandered from the

dust kicked up from a sandstorm swirling

around the wooden walls where I live alone.

Let me see your shape, outlined by the sun,

backing your body from behind as you approach

to change the plot of my chaste, missionary existence.

A charming Flame came to my door and asked to come inside.

He knocked as would a Gentleman, he wore a suit and tie.

His cologne smelled of embers and he tempted me to trust

his smooth and subtle slickness when he walked in and he
 brushed—

my hip so casually I felt a stir deep down.

And though it burned, his touch had churned some spark...
 without a sound.

And whether I know better, still, I let the Fire stay—

—it's not my heart— but— some other part...

that won't send him away.

 Not About Loss

I washed myself clean,

kneeling by the tub

and dipping my washcloth

in the warm water.

I saw steam breathing on the mirror,

felt the droplets dewing down my neck.

I smoothed the soap softly onto my body

beneath my breasts,

under my arms and

along the length of my legs.

When I was finished,

I poured the rest of the water over me;

so it fell in an avalanche of intimate liquid

sliding around my shoulders,

wrapping itself around my hips

in a hold reminiscent of hands.

TILTING AT WINDMILLS.

I want you like the wind wants
to twirl the blades of a windmill
round and round
until the friction forces the
energy out and into the
stem of the mechanism
buried deep
in the undergrounds of the earth
and when the dynamo reaches its
maximum capacity I'll burn out
all of my energy on you
and when our motors wind down
we'll spin listless
synchronizing our breathing
with the breeze

if I could capture the air around me

and distill it into a scent

it would be the same as the space

between the petals of a rose

She dug her hands into the snow, expecting cold.
Instead, she found a globe. A small circular shape,
emanating something similar to dying embers.
She set the thing in her lap and sat,
moving her hands over the silver surface;
feeling none of the frost around or on the ground.
Slow, even strokes... until the small glow became
a burst of brilliance. Blinding light. Winding white
rays across the river's glass.
Then she held it to her lips, kissed,
keeping it close in her coat.

Not About Loss

He took his son down to the edge of the water

and told him to look in. He said, "See, there's a stream

leading out into the ocean and another doubling back

onto that brook deep into the woods where your

mother and I met." He hoped someday his son would see

the same beauty as he. That he won't walk away from the

rivers or lakes or ripples and tides or currents carried, hidden

under the placid surface of the sleeping giants of nature.

So he took his son back to their home and he watched

as he grew by the river. And the thought of not knowing

consumed him. But all he could do was groom him,

so when he went out to the world he'd return to the water

alone.

WILDLAND.

Something more like
lightening,
I think.
And rather less
like wind
where one can't trace
the source of the flame.

Dawn, morning meets me.
She greets me in the kitchen;
pours cups of coffee.
And I sit and sip and sleep,
dreaming away the daylight.

MEET.

I'd say the voice
must sound something
like goodnight.
That word whispered
at the end
of some future Friday.

                    Not About Loss

Come find me in the dark

where I am sleeping all alone.

Say your name so I

will know it's you. And show

me the sign we made

when no one else was looking.

So I can see a reason

to trust the hands still searching;

feeling in the lack of light

till I reach out for you.

And hold your hand,

where tenseness— tight

you'll finally undo.

I yelled into a void and it threw back my voice;

the same sound repeated through eons and times before time.

And I shouted my musings across galaxies and over moons

until I wondered, how it was, even the faintest echo

could be heard in a vacuum—

But soon, faintly, another voice flew swiftly and mixed with

  mine

and the stardust.

Until (all at once) I knew I had hit on more than just an echo.

And I sent excited signals into space,

beeping my name

so it would be known and

never forgotten,

never forgotten...

I write messages in bottles

and send them across the ocean.

A word in each sentence for

all the days missed.

A sentence in each paragraph

for the passing months.

And numberless spaces between

the breaks and punctuation and

in the margins of the pages

that remind me—

of the miles still between.

- .. -- . .- -. -.. - .. -.. .

Though the tide has gone out

I cannot cross to the mainland.

So, I send my messages;

black and white stains on a

blank page...

They make me feel I'm doing

something with my idle time

other than— waiting.

Sitting and sending missives.

Every other letter receiving a reply.

Just to remind me—

you're alive.

VIRGINIA'S DEN.

I imagine a chair where

I have giant arms

to lean against

And a sense of

the welcoming winters

to come spent

in a Room of One's Own

I leave here and live here

and have left her

the woman I want to be

in that chair

sitting there

I envy the life she's living

No glory or fame

but just a chair that

touches her arms

strokes her back

supports her legs

at the end of

Life's weary day

I imagine this

Now and then

Not About Loss

DEN DREAM.

During the day I dreamt,
I dreamt while I was sleeping.
I heard a key in the door
and footsteps falling on the floor
and I tried to open my eyes,
but I slept so heavily they stayed shut.
And I was afraid until I felt
this spectre brush my hand.
Then it left— and I slept
and when I woke, I wondered
what was real.

WHEN WE SLEEP, I THINK.

Goodnight again— and we'll save
the conversations for tomorrow.
For now, we'll lie here holding
onto this tonight moment before
it disappears into a whisper.
So, say your silent goodnight.
I'll kiss you in the lamp light long
before our words wake up the sun.

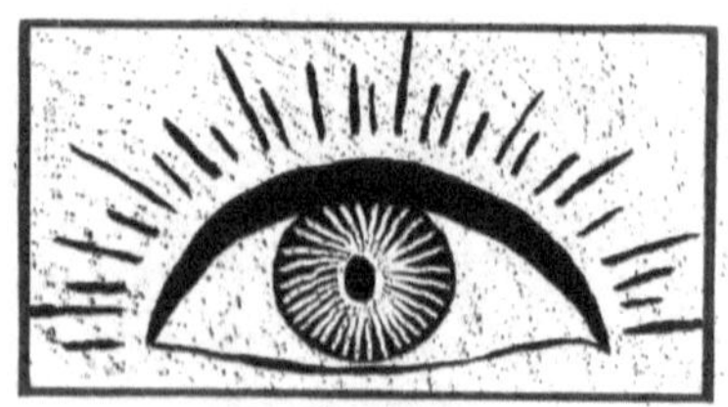

Not About Loss

iii.

NOT ABOUT LEMONS

∞

When she finished running she was in a whimsical mood:

"I think I'll say some nonsense."

"Well," said the tree, "What are you waiting for?"

WAKE.

I held a funeral for my handwriting
Even the Doctors could not save it

 Not About Lemons

OXFORD.

Three ships are passing in the night

a black, a white, and red

or are they passing in plain sight;

the black, the white and red?

Perhaps, it's two, not even three.

This simplifies the thread.

Which is it, Captain— bold and dashing?

Mayhap, A P misled...

PURPLE PENS.

This purple poem
penned from long-dried
ink stains on my moistened
and supple soul.
Haphazardly broken by
asteroids flung from
the darkest depths of spaces
between my ears.
A galactic message
in an incandescent bottle
shot into the atmosphere.
Only to disintegrate on impact
with an ever-loving touch.

Not About Lemons

URBANE DICTIONARY.

Tell all the truth but tell it yeet—
Success in Slang words lies
Too woke for our infirm D-lite
The Truth's dayum dank surprise
As Lit as all dem Hip Kidz be
Wut explanation find?
Dat troof jus dazzle gradually
Or erry bro be blind—

THAT ONE THAT RHYMES ABOUT THE SUN.

A poem about the sun is nothing new;

the warm and shining star in clouds above.

So often illustrated, here, in verse.

And in our allegories about love.

See, if I took the sun and held it close

it'd burn my hands and scorch the earth around.

I'd sooner sun myself more miles away

keeping my feet, still, safely on the ground.

Maybe that's why the moon comes out at night

to offer us a place to bare all "me."

Then otherwise all us in plain sight

too much for that harsh sun to want to see.

The heat I'll take in hours at a time,

but evening I will bask as if it's mine.

     Not About Lemons

MR. WEBSTER.

A comma and quotation mark
were fighting to be first.
"Oh, I should be! Not you, but ME!"
No rule for which was worse.
For some will tell you that it's fine
"To pen your sents like so,"
but others have another plan
for how this match should go.
The heavy-handed Quoteteers
would push "this version hard",
harsh-R'd Comma Commanders have
colonial regard.
So, really, what's the answer here?
And what began the fight?
...those fumbling compositors
got too damn drunk one night...

BLEEDING INK.

Poets
A group of people who
think that
they're the only ones who
listened to
Somebody That I Used To Know
on repeat
after a breakup

Another speaker in her head said,

"Don't take yourself so seriously.

After all, gold is dug from dirt."

"Clever," she replied.

She stood to walk toward home;

thinking less of those deep things.

And stepped, barefoot, onto the grass.

www.ingramcontent.com/pod-product-compliance
Lightning Source LLC
Chambersburg PA
CBHW032130050726
47590CB00008B/3035